Karlene Harvey is an illustrator and writer, and she lives on the unceded and ancestral home territories of the Musqueam, Squamish and Tsleil-Waututh people. She is Tŝilhqot'in through her mother and Syilx through her father, both sides of her family include a mix of European ancestry. Following her studies at Emily Carr Institute of Art and Design, she pursued an illustration practice that was inspired by zine and underground comic culture, independent animation and collage art. In recent years, she is invested in representation and how to best depict diverse peoples within her drawings. Her work has been published by a number of arts and culture magazines and can be found in the publication #NotyourNDNPrincess. She is currently completing a Master of Arts degree in English Literature with a specific focus on Indigenous literature at the University of British Columbia.

karleneharvey.com

"This book is dedicated to those who attended Residential School and never had the opportunity to learn their culture. I drum from the heart for you."

Project Manager: Kaitlyn Stampflee
Design: Eden Sunflower
Editor: Kaitlyn Stampflee
ISBN: 978-1-989122-88-4
Printed in PRC.
Published in Canada by Medicine Wheel Education.
For more book information go to www.medicinewheel.education

Funded by the Government of Canada   Financé par le gouvernement du Canada

DRUM FROM THE HEART

Author: Ren Louie
Illustrator: Karlene Harvey

On a beautiful summer day, six-year-old Ren waited patiently at home for his cousins to arrive. His family was preparing a lunch, and many relatives were invited.

When his family finally arrived, Ren noticed his cousin was carrying a little drum. Round, with a nice golden-brown colour, a wooden rim, and only one drumstick, Ren knew this drum was special and not at all like the drums he had seen in a local marching band.

Curious and intrigued by this new drum, Ren turned to his Grandmother to ask, "Grandma, do you know what that drum is made of?" Ren's grandmother replied, "The drum is made from deer hide, and the rim of the drum and the drumstick are both made of yellow cedar."

Imagining all of the stories a traditional drum like this could tell, Ren was excited to learn about this one.
"In our Nuu-chah-nulth language, we refer to the drum as a Cukáʕ (koot-yuk)," his grandmother taught him.

Ren and his cousin took turns playing with the golden-brown drum. Ren, smiling from ear to ear, joyfully played the drum using a wooden spatula with a red sock on the end while his cousin used the yellow cedar drumstick. They had so much fun listening to all of the different sounds they could make with their mismatched drumsticks.

With the cousins happily drumming, Ren's grandmother, while clapping along, began to sing. Ren's cousin, confident and proud with his deer hide drum in hand, joined in to sing along to the traditional song from his nation. Ren wished he could proudly sing this traditional song, but he was much too shy.

As his family prepared to leave, Ren felt sad that he did not have the confidence to sing along with his grandmother and cousin like he wanted to.

A few years later on his ninth birthday, Ren was gifted a drum, handmade by his mother. This handmade drum, while it looked a lot like the drum his cousin had, was made especially for him. This was the first drum made by his mother, which made it even more special.

When she gave him the drum, Ren's mother said, "My son, I want you to have your very own drum. It will help you as you learn how to sing. Then you too can feel confident enough to share the gift of your voice with others."

The drum, strikingly beautiful with a blue and red salmon design, filled Ren with so much pride as he played it for the first time. Boom! Boom! Boom!

After covering her ears, Ren's mom reminded him that he should take care of his new drum by being gentle and tapping it lightly.

"The drum represents your heartbeat, boom-boom, boom-boom, boom-boom. You must take care of this drum and respect it," she told him. "You don't ever want to set the drum face down. To warm it up, you'll hold it close to the fire. If there is no fire, you'll warm it up by hugging the front of the drum to your chest." Ren listened closely as his mother demonstrated her teachings.

Ren was so happy to have his very own drum
that he gave his mom the biggest hug a
nine-year-old could give.

Excited by the promise of what this new drum might teach him, Ren joined a drumming group in his community. Every week, with his beautiful blue and red painted salmon drum in one hand and his own yellow cedar drumstick in the other, Ren learned to drum.

In the beginning, while other members of the group enthusiastically sang along while they drummed, Ren still felt much too shy to share his voice with the others.

Over time, the bond between Ren and his drum began to grow.
The more he would drum, the more confident and
proud he became.

While rehearsing for an upcoming parade that his new drum group would soon participate in, Ren's grandmother watched closely. At the rehearsal, Ren was surprised when he was given the chance to sing a solo. Hesitant at first, but with his beloved drum in hand, Ren began to sing... very quietly.

Although quiet, Ren's singing was very delightful to his grandmother. It reminded her of her father and uncles, who also sang these same traditional songs. It made her so happy to finally hear Ren singing them too.

Before very long, Ren came to realize just how much he actually loved singing!

On the day of the big parade, with his mother on one side and his grandmother on the other, Ren was filled with pride. Head held high, and arms reached strongly out front, he proudly sang as he marched to the beat of his prized drum. Along with his drum, Ren carried pride for his family, pride for his community, and pride for his culture.

With his newfound confidence after the parade, Ren was excited when he returned to school. His teacher, who was also in the drum group, held weekly assemblies in class, and Ren was actually looking forward to singing.

Encouraged by Ren, his friends and classmates participated too. One by one, they all took turns singing. Knowing just how afraid it can make you feel to share your voice with others, Ren was so happy to see his friends drumming and singing along!

As Ren grew up, his treasured gift grew with him.
Ren's handmade golden-brown drum, still beautifully painted with
colours of bright red and blue, continues to remind him of the love
of his mother and grandmother. It reminds him to always be proud
of who he is and where he comes from.

Grateful for the teachings he was given as a child, Ren now shares
these same teachings with other children. With his favourite drum
still by his side, Ren keeps his culture strong by showing children how
to be courageous and practice their own culture, just like he does.

MEDICINE WHEEL
EDUCATION

www.medicinewheel.education

Online Courses Available:
www.classroom.medicinewheel.education

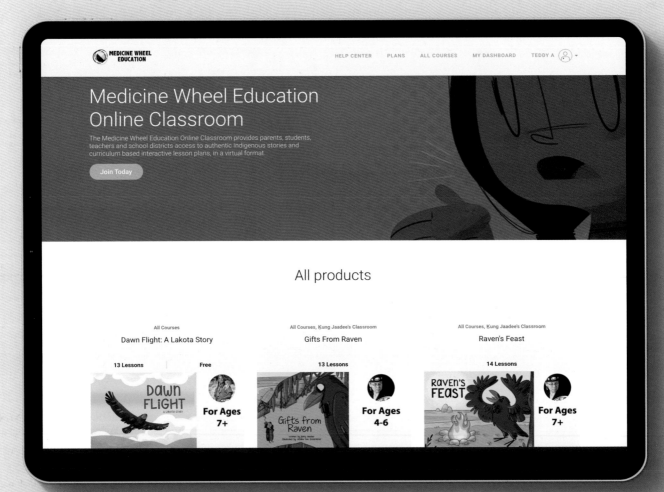